United by Love: The Mother-Daughter Journal - Bridging Gaps Through Generations!

This book belongs to

_____

and

_____

Date _____

Mom and Daughter, welcome to the first page of your journal. Get ready for a journey that's uniquely yours!

How To Approach Tasks in This Journal

Be ready to dedicate 10–15 minutes of uninterrupted time for each activity. We strongly encourage you to work through the activities together, as some pages will require you to reflect and have a conversation. You can either look through the pages and choose activities that resonate with you both at that moment, or you can build a habit of filling it out daily page by page – it's up to you.

Build an Emotional Connection

Make sure to be in tune and present by putting off all distractions and becoming attuned to each other's thoughts. Take extra time to have a conversation with each other and ask leading questions. This journal is perfect for finding a sense of peace after a long day. Watch your emotions transform into valuable lessons, establishing the foundation of personal growth and positive thinking. Take this experience a step further by writing notes about your insights at the margins of the pages and incorporating the practices and lessons in your daily life.

Communicate with Kindness, not Harshness

This journal promotes the idea of empathy, which is the ability to understand and share the feelings of others. It emphasizes the importance of appreciating different viewpoints and recognizing the distinct qualities and values that each person possesses. By doing so, it aims to foster a sense of understanding and respect among individuals, which can lead to more harmonious and compassionate relationships.

Respect Boundaries and Show Appreciation

The journal will also guide you on the importance of building relationships based on mutual respect and trust. It suggests showing gratitude for each other's actions, having open discussions about providing support during challenging times, and celebrating successes together. Additionally, it highlights the significance of respecting each other's boundaries, which is crucial for maintaining a healthy and balanced relationship. Remember to write down valuable lessons, words of encouragement, and appreciation to each other on the margins of the journal.

Integrating the Mindfulness

Being mindful is essential for empathy and social interactions, helping daughters to build healthy relationships. The book will teach you to integrate those reflective moments and activities into your daily life. For example, asking each other questions and getting feedback, dealing with emotions in a healthy way, and giving each other affirmations. As you fill out the pages, you'll notice that some mindful practices are especially enjoyable and helpful, having the potential to become a regular part of your routine. Remember, in these simple exercises lies the magic of connection and growth.

The Only Rule: There Are No Rules!

This book is filled with inspiration and tools for you to enjoy. Use it however you wish without feeling bound to follow every entry. Feel free to modify, skip, or even create entirely new activities. The journal is yours to shape and adapt its activities as you see fit.

Most importantly, don't stress!

Remember, this is about taking small steps and focusing on the present. Some of the topics may seem overwhelming, but you'll be surprised at what you can achieve by sharing your thoughts and emotions with each other!

Now, you're ready to start your adventure. Turn to the next page!

Me, Right Now

Daughter, grab a recent selfie or photo you feel represents you and paste it right in the center!

⭐ Paste your chosen photo here!

Name: _____

Nickname: _____

Birthday: _____

Your favorite way to connect with your Mom:

_____

What's trending for you? (music, fashion, etc.):

_____

Your signature style (color, clothing, etc.):

_____

Passions & pastimes:

_____

Current favorite series:

_____

Favorite social media or gaming platform:

_____

Influencers or role models:

_____

One thing i want to change in the world:

_____

Likes: _____

Dislikes: _____

Mom, grab a recent selfie or photo you feel represents you and paste it right in the center!
⭐ Paste your chosen photo here!

Name: _____
You're Known For (a skill, a saying, a role):
_____
Your Favorite Way to Connect with Your Daughter:
_____
Proudest Mom Moment:
_____
A Lesson Learned from Parenting:
_____
Favorite Way to Unwind:
_____
One Thing You've Mastered This Year:
_____
A Book That Moved You:
_____
Your Go-To Comfort Food:
_____
Hopes for Your Daughter:
_____
A Personal Goal: _____
Likes: _____
Dislikes: _____

Family Trivia

Mom, grab your journal and a pen. Daughter, get a separate piece of paper for your guesses. Daughter, when Mom asks a question, write down your answer on your paper. No peeking at the journal! Mom, write down the actual answers in your journal. Keep it hidden until the end of the game. Once all the questions have been asked and answered, transfer the daughter's guesses to the table and compare them to your responses. How many did she get right?

	What is the Daughter's guess?	Correct Answer	Did she get it right?
Mom's favorite meal			
A place Mom wants to travel			
A game Mom likes to play the most			
A book Mom has read recently			
Mom's favorite celebrity			
Where did Mom work for her very first job?			
Which subject was Mom's strongest back in her school days?			
What's one thing Mom always does to start her day?			
What's one meal Mom cooks better than anyone else?			
What was the first pet Mom ever had?			

Daughter, now it's your turn to ask questions. Grab your journal and a pen. Mom, get a separate piece of paper for your guesses. Mom, when Daughter asks a question, write your answer on your paper. No peeking at the journal!
Daughter, write down the actual answers in your journal. Keep it hidden until the end of the game. Once all the questions have been asked and answered, transfer Mom's guesses to the table and compare them to your responses. How many did she get right?

	What is your Mom's guess?	Correct Answer	Did she get it right?
Daughter's favorite meal			
A place your Daughter wants to travel			
A game your Daughter likes to play the most.			
A book your Daughter has read recently.			
Your Daughter's favorite celebrity			
Which birthday does your Daughter remember most fondly, and what made it special?			
Which subject was/is your Daughter's strongest in school?			
What's one thing your Daughter always does to start her day?			
What's one meal your Daughter cooks better than anyone else?			
Did your Daughter attend any concerts? Who did she see for her first live concert?			

Grand Award

Daughter, would you like to be famous? Why or why not?

_____

_____

_____

Imagine you happen to become famous for your achievements. What did you do to become well-known? Are you an artist, a scientist, a leader, or something entirely different?

_____

_____

Take a moment to visualize a scene where you are giving an interview or a speech after receiving an award for your achievement. Share your story.
What made you choose this kind of fame?

_____

_____

_____

What struggles did you overcome?

_____

_____

_____

How do you think becoming famous in this way would change your life or other people's lives?

_____

_____

_____

Mom, would you like to be famous? Why or why not?

_____

_____

_____

Imagine you happen to become famous for your achievements. What did you do to become well-known? Are you an artist, a scientist, a leader, or something entirely different?

_____

_____

Take a moment to visualize a scene where you are giving an interview or a speech after receiving an award for your achievement. Share your story.
What made you choose this kind of fame?

_____

_____

_____

What struggles did you overcome?

_____

_____

_____

How do you think becoming famous in this way would change your life or other people's lives?

_____

_____

_____

Mom & Me
Adventure Checklist

Daughter, here's a checklist of fun and memorable activities to explore with your Mom. As you experience these adventures together, tick them off the list. Which of these have you already enjoyed together?

- ☐ Skiing or roller skating
- ☐ Visiting the beach
- ☐ Watching a movie at the cinema
- ☐ Having a picnic
- ☐ Going shopping
- ☐ Hosting a game night or a potluck dinner
- ☐ Baking homemade cookies
- ☐ Attending a masterclass
- ☐ Singing at karaoke
- ☐ Playing mini golf
- ☐ Creating a painting together
- ☐ Participating in a quiz night
- ☐ Making a scrapbook
- ☐ Playing video games
- ☐ Exploring a new city
- ☐ Practicing yoga
- ☐ Go camping or take a hide
- ☐ Volunteer
- ☐ Have a garage sale or sell things you don't need
- ☐ Go for a bike ride
- ☐ Homemade pizza
- ☐ Visit a gallery or a museum
- ☐ Learn a new skill
- ☐ Visit a family member
- ☐ Make a photobook
- ☐ Movie night and face mask
- ☐ Visit a beauty salon

Daughter, what's new adventures or experiences you want to share with your Mom?

Mom, what's new adventures or experiences you want to share with your Daughter?

Favorite Memory

Daughter, draw or write about your favorite memory of you and your Mom. Compare and reflect on those memories with her.

Why does this particular memory stand out to you? What does this memory make you feel?

_____

_____

_____

What is your favorite way to spend time as a family?

_____

_____

_____

Mom, draw or write about your favorite memory of you and your Daughter. Compare and reflect on those memories with her.

Why does this particular memory stand out to you? What does this memory make you feel?

What is your favorite way to spend time as a family?

Choose this or that

Get to know the little and big things about your thoughts and feelings. Take turns answering the questions and explaining your choice. There's no rush, so feel free to laugh, debate, and dive deep into each choice.

	Mom	Daughter
Would you prefer a button to rewind life or pause it at will?		
Where are you happiest: in bustling city streets or the peaceful countryside?		
Choose to be wealthy or well-known.		
Would you rather be known as the funniest or the most intelligent person in a room?		
Would you prefer a private proposal or one with family and friends?		
Would you rather win a massive lottery or have the opportunity to double your lifespan?		

	Mom	Daughter	17
Would you prefer to have the power to alter the past or the ability to foresee the future?			
Would you rather meet your ancestors from 100 years ago or your descendants 100 years into the future?			
Where would you be if you could be anywhere in the world?			
What would you change about your personality if you could choose one thing?			
Would you rather spend your free time hiking in the mountains or relaxing on the beach?			
Which season do you look forward to more: summer's warmth or winter's coziness?			

Family Ties

Daughter,

Reflect on the benefits of having a close-knit family. How does this bond support you in life, provide a sense of security, or simply lighten up your day?

_____

_____

_____

Recall a cherished memory with an older family member. What moment with them brings a smile to your face?

_____

_____

_____

Contemplate the meaning of 'family.' Does it refer strictly to blood relations, or does it encompass the friends who are always there for you, or perhaps something else entirely?

_____

_____

_____

Consider who in your family is notably unique or eccentric. What is it about them that stands out to you?

_____

_____

_____

Think back to a visit with your extended family that you really enjoyed. What made that gathering or visit unforgettable for you?

_____

_____

_____

Discuss your shared memories with your Mom. Reflect on how each of you recalls these events — what details do you remember differently, and which moments do you both hold dear?

_____

_____

_____

Mom,

Reflect on the benefits of having a close-knit family. How does this bond support you in life, provide a sense of security, or simply lighten up your day?

_____

_____

_____

Recall a cherished memory with an older family member. What moment with them brings a smile to your face?

_____

_____

_____

Contemplate the meaning of 'family.' Does it refer strictly to blood relations, or does it encompass the friends who are always there for you, or perhaps something else entirely?

_____

_____

_____

Consider who in your family is notably unique or eccentric. What is it about them that stands out to you?

_____

_____

_____

Think back to a visit with your extended family that you really enjoyed. What made that gathering or visit unforgettable for you?

_____

_____

_____

Discuss your shared memories with your Daughter. Reflect on how each of you recalls these events —what details do you remember differently, and which moments do you both hold dear?

_____

_____

_____

Special Powers

Daughter, what do you think your Mom's real-life superpower is?

_____
_____
_____
_____
_____
_____

What other job would be suitable for your Mom?

_____
_____
_____
_____
_____
_____

What qualities or talents make her perfect for that career?

_____
_____
_____
_____
_____
_____

Mom, what do you think your Daughter's real-life superpower is?

_____

_____

_____

_____

_____

_____

What job would be suitable for your Daughter?

_____

_____

_____

_____

_____

_____

What qualities or talents make her perfect for that career?

_____

_____

_____

_____

_____

_____

My Growth Journey

Daughter, think about your biggest achievements or something important you're working on.

★ What goals have you set in the past that you are working on?
★ What other goals do you have? Are they similar to your Mom's or different?

_____
_____
_____
_____

★ What successes have you had? Has progress been made since you set the goal? What intermediate results have you achieved?
★ Is there something that led you to this, like useful habits?

_____
_____
_____
_____

★ What will be a reward or a good result from your goals?
★ Are you willing to stop or move to the next milestone after you finish this one?

_____
_____
_____
_____

Mom, think about your biggest achievements or something important you're working on.

★ What goals have you set in the past that you are working on?
★ What other goals do you have? Are they similar to your Daughter's or different?

_____
_____
_____
_____

★ What successes have you had? Has progress been made since you set the goal? What intermediate results have you achieved?
★ Is there something that led you to this, like useful habits?

_____
_____
_____
_____

★ What will be a reward or a good result from your goals?
★ Are you willing to stop or move to the next milestone after you finish this one?

_____
_____
_____
_____

Life's Crossroads

Daughter, the path in the picture represents different life choices, with dead-ends and clear paths leading to various outcomes. These crossroads represent specific instances where you had to choose between saying "yes" or "no."

Describe one scenario where you said "yes".

How did your choice influence your life?

What would have happened if you h said "no"?

Think about a time you said "no" to something.

What led to that decision?

Do you wish you had said yes, or are you glad you said "no"?

Do you have specific rules or limits for when to say "no" or "yes" to people or choices in life? Talk about your criteria with your Mom and reflect.

_____

_____

_____

Mom, the path in the picture represents different life choices, with dead-ends and clear paths leading to various outcomes. These crossroads represent specific instances where you had to choose between saying "yes" or "no."

Describe one scenario where you said "yes".

w did your choice influence your life?

What would have happened if you had said "no"?

Think about a time you said "no" to something.

What led to that decision?

Do you wish you had said yes, or are you glad you said "no"?

Do you have specific rules or limits for when to say "no" or "yes" to people or choices in life? Talk about your criteria with your Daughter and reflect.

_____

_____

_____

Mom's Past

Daughter,

Which clubs or organizations was your Mom a part of in high school or college? What were her goals at that time? Ask her and learn more about her experiences.

_____

_____

_____

_____

_____

_____

What aspects of your Mom's life story do you find fascinating? Are there any memories from her life you wish you could experience yourself?

_____

_____

_____

_____

_____

_____

Mom,

Which year of your life so far has been your favorite? Why?

_____
_____
_____
_____
_____
_____
_____

Have you achieved all the goals you set for yourself in childhood, and which goals have changed?

_____
_____
_____
_____
_____
_____

Mom, do you think everyone has a calling? Have you found yours?

_____
_____
_____
_____
_____
_____

Daughter's Past

Describe the day your Daughter was born. How did you prepare for it?

_____

_____

_____

Were there any challenges you faced while raising your Daughter?

_____

_____

_____

What quirky thing did your Daughter do as a child?

_____

_____

_____

What was the most rewarding thing about raising your Daughter?

_____

_____

_____

Daughter,

What is one of your earliest childhood memories? Describe it.

_____

_____

_____

What was your favorite childhood hobby or activity, and do you still enjoy it today?

_____

_____

_____

Do you remember a place from childhood that holds a special place in your heart? What is special about it?

_____

_____

_____

What was your favorite fantasy world or dream from your childhood that you frequently imagined?

_____

_____

_____

The Emotional Avocado

Daughter, imagine your personality as an avocado. The flesh represents your positive traits, while the seed symbolizes aspects you might want to improve. Reflect on two situations: one where you behaved at your best and where you wish you could have acted better.

Describe the situation where you behaved your best.

What positive traits did you exhibit in that situation?

Describe the situation where you wish you could have acted better.

What negative traits did you exhibit in that situation?

In what ways are you and your Mom different and similar? Did you and your Mom experience similar situations? Did you resolve them in the same way?

Why did you exhibit these negative emotions or traits? Did they help you adapt and get out of the situation?

Was there a realization that you went too far? How did you act after that? Did you apologize or rectify the situation?

Mom, imagine your personality as an avocado. The flesh represents your positive traits, while the seed symbolizes aspects you might want to improve. Reflect on two situations: one where you behaved at your best and where you wish you could have acted better.

Describe the situation where you behaved your best.

What positive traits did you exhibit in that situation?

Describe the situation where you wish you could have acted better.

What negative traits did you exhibit in that situation?

In what ways are you and your Daughter different and similar? Did you and your Daughter experience similar situations? Did you resolve them in the same way?

Why did you exhibit these negative emotions or traits? Did they help you adapt and get out of the situation?

Was there a realization that you went too far? How did you act after that? Did you apologize or rectify the situation?

Mom, imagine you're describing your Daughter to someone who doesn't know her by answering the questions below!

Think about the qualities that make her stand out, her personality and the energy she brings to a room. What makes her unique in your eyes?

_____

_____

_____

What do friends and family say about her energy and presence?

_____

_____

_____

Describe the aspects of her heart and soul that might not be immediately visible to others. Consider her kindness, resilience, honesty, or any traits you admire. What does she care deeply about? How does she show love and compassion?

_____

_____

_____

Reflect on how she has grown over the years. How has she evolved in her thinking, aspirations, or approach to life?

_____

_____

_____

Daughter, imagine you're describing your Mom to someone who doesn't know her by answering the questions below!

Think about the qualities that make her stand out, her personality and the energy she brings to a room. What makes her unique in your eyes? What do friends and family say about her energy and presence?

_____

_____

_____

Describe the aspects of her heart and soul that might not be immediately visible to others. Consider her kindness, resilience, honesty, or any traits you admire. What does she care deeply about? How does she show love and compassion?

_____

_____

_____

Reflect on how the image of your Mom has changed in your eyes. What qualities or traits does your Mom possess that you have come to appreciate more over time?

_____

_____

_____

Shared Sky Constellation

Mom and Daughter,
Each star on this page symbolizes things that make you and your Mom unique, so write down each of these things near the star. This can include:

- **Looks:** Maybe you have curly hair, you're really tall, or you have a smile that lights up the room.
- **Personality:** Are you super friendly? Maybe you're the brave one in the group, or you're known for being really patient.
- **Hobbies:** What do you love to do? It could be painting, playing soccer, coding computer games, or gardening.
- **Dreams:** Think about what hope you have for the future. Do you dream of traveling the world, starting your own business, or maybe inventing something cool?

After you finish, connect the traits and interests you both share to form your unique constellation. Come up with a creative name for your constellation.

_____

_____

_____

Mom, what would you have never gotten into but did because of your Daughter?

_____

_____

_____

_____

Get to Know Each Other Better

Mom,
What would be the perfect gift for you?

_____

Is there a movie that you could rewatch again and again times?
If so, which one?

_____

What band or a singer defined your teenage years?

_____

What would you do with $1,000?

_____

What's the last thing you completed on your bucket list?

_____

What's your favorite family tradition?

_____

Which season fits your personality best?

_____

What is your favorite getaway place?

_____

What is your favorite way to work out?

_____

Daughter,
What would be the perfect gift for you?

_____

Is there a movie that you could rewatch again and again?
If so, which one?

_____

What band or a singer defines your teenage years?

_____

What would you do with $1,000?

_____

What's the last thing you completed on your bucket list?

_____

What's your favorite family tradition?

_____

Which season fits your personality best?

_____

What is your favorite getaway place?

_____

What is your favorite way to work out?

_____

Personal Boundaries Map

Daughter, what do personal boundaries mean to you? Use the diagram to answer questions about the layers of your personality that you're willing to share with the world. Each layer represents different social circles in your life.

- -

Core: What do you keep private?
Outer Core: What do you share with family and friends?
Mantle: What do you share with schoolmates, colleagues, or neighbors?
Crust: What do you share online or with people you don't know?

- -

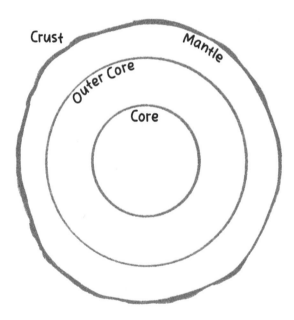

How do you communicate your needs and boundaries to others?

_____

_____

In what ways do you think your Mom can support your independence while still being involved in your life? Write quick notes on how you gu can respect each other's space and what you share with .

_____

_____

Mom, what do personal boundaries mean to you? Use the diagram to answer questions about the layers of your personality that you're willing to share with the world. Each layer represents different social circles in your life.

Core: What do you keep private?
Outer Core: What do you share with family and friends?
Mantle: What do you share with schoolmates, colleagues, or neighbors?
Crust: What do you share online or with people you don't know?

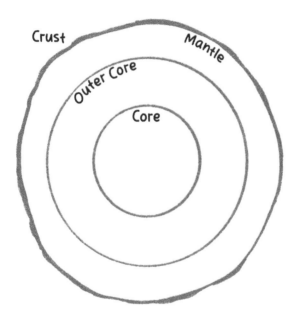

How do you perceive the concept of boundaries in your relationship with your Daughter?

_____

_____

Reflecting on your own experiences at your daughter's age, how do you relate to her need for personal boundaries?

_____

_____

What steps can you take to ensure you respect your daughter's boundaries and provide her with the support she needs?

_____

_____

Opening Up

Daughter,
Can you share a time from your recent life or childhood when you felt embarrassed? How do you feel about sharing this experience — is it still awkward, or have you moved past those feelings?

_____

_____

_____

What lessons did you learn from this experience?

_____

_____

_____

Can you recall the last time you cried and why?

_____

_____

_____

Discuss with your Mom how you can cope with this situation and avoid similar ones in the future and how she might assist you. Write your notes here. In what ways could your Mom have supported you through the aftermath of this experience, or how can she help in such moments moving forward?

_____

_____

_____

Daughter's Support

Mom,
Do you think you have experienced significant changes in your life in recent years? What are they?

_____

_____

_____

What's the most challenging choice you've ever had to make, and who or what helped in this process?

_____

_____

_____

Do these changes teach you something? In what way? What piece of advice can you give to your Daughter?

_____

_____

_____

What does your Daughter do to add more happiness to your daily life?

_____

_____

_____

When do you need your Daughter's support and attention, and in what ways?

_____

_____

_____

Our Best Day

Daughter, think about how you can plan out your day so it will be favorable for you in the near future. What does a very productive day look like for you? Start from the moment you wake up until you go to bed.

Time	Activity
_____	_____
_____	_____
_____	_____
_____	_____
_____	_____
_____	_____
_____	_____
_____	_____
_____	_____
_____	_____
_____	_____
_____	_____
_____	_____

What new habits should you adopt and implement in your life tomorrow? For example, setting a consistent wake-up time or dedicating specific hours to focused work.

_____

_____

_____

Discuss how your Mom can support you in achieving these goals. Be open to adjustments. Your Mom might have insights or suggestions to refine your plans or propose new habits you hadn't considered.

Reflect on the similarities and differences between your goals and habits and those of your Mom. What are the activities you can share?

_____

_____

_____

_____

Mom, think about how you can plan out your day so it will be favorable for you in the near future. What does a very productive day look like for you? Start from the moment you wake up until you go to bed.

Time	Activity

What new habits should you adopt and implement in your life tomorrow? For example, setting a consistent wake-up time or dedicating specific hours to focused work.

_____

_____

_____

Discuss how your Daugther can support you in achieving these goals. Be open to adjustments. Your Daugther might have insights or suggestions to refine your plans or propose new habits you hadn't considered.

Reflect on the similarities and differences between your goals and habits and those of your Daughter. What are the activities you can share?

_____

_____

_____

_____

Love Story

Mom, share a love story about your family or closest friends.

_____
_____
_____
_____
_____
_____
_____
_____
_____
_____
_____
_____
_____
_____
_____
_____
_____
_____
_____
_____
_____
_____

Daughter

How did the story make you feel? Does any part of it really stick with you?

_____

_____

_____

How could a love story like this happen in today's world? Would things play out differently with how we date and communicate now?

_____

_____

_____

What values do you think were most important to the couple in the story? Loyalty, passion, compromise? How do those values align with what you believe is vital in a relationship?

_____

_____

_____

If you could extract one key takeaway from this love story to guide you in your future or present relationships, what would it be?

_____

_____

_____

How has hearing this story influenced your understanding of intimacy and commitment?

_____

_____

_____

Overcoming Fears

Mom, what do you think is your Daughter's biggest fear?

_____

_____

_____

What advice can you give to help your Daughter overcome her fear?

_____

_____

_____

What's the most daring thing you've ever done? Describe a time when you faced and overcame your fear.

_____

_____

_____

Have fears ever stopped you from completing something?

_____

_____

_____

Daughter, what do you think is your Mom's biggest fear? Ask her more adout it.

_____

_____

_____

What advice can you give to help your Mom overcome her fear?

_____

_____

_____

What's the most daring thing you've ever done? Describe a time when you faced and overcame your fear.

_____

_____

_____

Have fears ever stopped you from completing something?

_____

_____

_____

Role models

Mom, who was your role model growing up? Why?

_____

_____

_____

_____

_____

Which teacher had the most significant influence on you, and why?

_____

_____

_____

_____

_____

Do you and your Daughter share any similarities in the people you look up to?

_____

_____

_____

_____

_____

Daughter, who is your main role model? Why?

_____

_____

_____

_____

_____

Which teacher has had the most significant influence on you, and why?

_____

_____

_____

_____

_____

Do you and your Mom share any similarities in the people you look up to?

_____

_____

_____

_____

_____

Kindness

Daughter, what's the most heartwarming thing you've ever seen or experienced?

_____

_____

_____

_____

_____

What was the nicest thing anyone has ever said to you?

_____

_____

_____

_____

_____

What kind of things does your Mom do to make you feel loved and appreciated?

_____

_____

_____

_____

_____

Mom, what's the most heartwarming thing you've ever seen?

_____
_____
_____
_____
_____

What was the nicest thing anyone has ever said to you?

_____
_____
_____
_____
_____

What kind of things does your Daughter do to make you feel loved and appreciated?

_____
_____
_____
_____
_____

Cherished Connections

Daughter, do you have any friends you consider family? Who are the dearest people in your life?

_____
_____
_____
_____

What's your favorite memory of you and your friends? Why?

_____
_____
_____
_____

Who knows the most about you?

_____
_____
_____
_____

What traits do you think are most important in a partner?

_____
_____
_____
_____

Mom, do you have any friends you consider family? Who are the dearest people in your life?

_____

_____

_____

_____

What's your favorite memory of you and your friends? Why?

_____

_____

_____

_____

Who knows the most about you?

_____

_____

_____

_____

What traits do you think are most important in a partner?

_____

_____

_____

_____

Gratitude jar

Daughter, take a moment to think about the things you are most grateful for in your life. These can be people, experiences, achievements, or simple everyday pleasures.

Inside the jar on your journal page, begin to draw hearts or any shapes you like. Each shape will represent a specific memory or aspect of your life that fills you with gratitude. Write a brief note about the memory or thing you're grateful for within each heart or shape. If the space is too small, you can number each shape and write the corresponding details beside the jar. Next, use your colored pens or pencils to fill and decorate the hearts or shapes.

Mom, take a moment to think about the things you are most grateful for in your life. These can be people, experiences, achievements, or simple everyday pleasures.

Inside the jar on your journal page, begin to draw hearts or any shapes you like. Each shape will represent a specific memory or aspect of your life that fills you with gratitude. Write a brief note about the memory or thing you're grateful for within each heart or shape. If the space is too small, you can number each shape and write the corresponding details beside the jar. Next, use your colored pens or pencils to fill and decorate the hearts or shapes.

Life's Chapters

Daughter, look at the four squares in your journal. These represent significant phases of your life so far. Think about key periods like early childhood, starting school, becoming a teenager, and now. Give those chapters a name. In each square, jot down the main events, obstacles, or experiences during that life phase.

Write a word or a short phrase about how you moved from one phase to the next. Did you feel excited, nervous, or maybe totally ready for it?

Name main events!

How did you feel adout moving to the new chapter of your life?

Name main events!

How did you feel adout moving to the new chapter of your life?

Name main events!

How did you feel adout moving to the new chapter of your life?

Name main events!

Mother, look at the four squares in your journal. These represent significant phases of your life so far. Think about key periods like graduating from school/college, having a favorite job, motherhood and now. Give those chapters a name. In each square, jot down the main events, obstacles or experiences during that life phase.
Write a word or a short phrase about how you moved from one phase to the next. Did you feel excited, nervous, or maybe totally ready for it?

Name main events!

How did you feel adout moving to the new chapter of your life?

Name main events!

How did you feel adout moving to the new chapter of your life?

Name main events!

How did you feel adout moving to the new chapter of your life?

Name main events!

In Each Other's Shoes

Imagine a day when you switch roles. Mom becomes the student, heading off to school or college, and the Daughter becomes the Mom for a day.

Mom,
what amazing feelings and memories would you experience in school or college again?

_____
_____
_____
_____
_____
_____

Mom, what moments or situations would you prefer to avoid if you went back to school or college?

_____
_____
_____
_____
_____
_____

Imagine a day when you switch roles. Mom becomes the student,
heading off to school or college, and the Daughter becomes the
Mom for a day.

Daughter, what fun and amazing things would you experience caring
for a child for a day?

_____
_____
_____
_____
_____
_____

Daughter, what challenges do you think you'd face taking care of a
child for a day?

_____
_____
_____
_____
_____

Unpacking Past Experiences

Daughter, think back to a challenging moment in your life, maybe when you were hurt or felt unsure or uncomfortable. This could be because of trouble in school/work, in relationships with people around you, or anything that bothers you. Write about a situation that happened in a few words.

_____

_____

In the first suitcase, name the emotions you "packed" after this event. It could be fear, anger, self-doubt, or something else. How did this situation affect you? How did it impact your self-esteem?

In the other suitcase write your reflection, what you learned from this experience, something positive.

How can you avoid avoid this situation from happening again or protect myself or others?

_____

_____

Reflect with your Mom about how she can support you emotionally and be there for you when you feel stressed. How can she help you physically, whether it's through taking care of your health or being present in your daily life?

_____

_____

Mother, think back to a challenging moment in your life, maybe when you were hurt or felt unsure or uncomfortable. This could be because of trouble in school/work, in relationships with people around you, or anything that bothers you. Write about a situation that happened in a few words.

_____

_____

n the first suitcase, name the emotions
ou "packed" after this event. It could be
ear, anger, self-doubt, or something else.
low did this situation affect you? How
id it impact your self-esteem?

In the other suitcase write your reflection, what you learned from this experience, something positive.

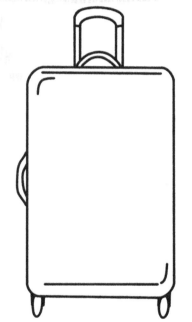 

How can you avoid avoid this situation from happening again or protect myself or others?

_____

_____

Reflect with your Daughter about how she can support you emotionally and be there for you when you feel stressed. How can she help you physically, whether it's through taking care of your health or being present in your daily life?

_____

_____

My Inner Tree of Strength

Daughter, did you face any challenges in your life, for example, in school, work, or relationships? How did you overcome them? Write them down near the gusts of wind.

Remember, your will is strong like a tree because you've got roots of support, like people or your strong inner qualities and talents. What are they? Write them down near the tree roots.

Challenges

What is your support?

Mom, did you face any challenges in your life, for example, in school, work, or relationships? How did you overcome them? Write them down near the gusts of wind.
Remember, your will is strong like a tree because you've got roots of support, like people or your strong inner qualities and talents. What are they? Write them down near the tree roots.

Challenges

What is your support?

The Blossoming Journey

Mom, if your Daughter was a flower, what flower would she be?

Drawing Instructions:
Draw a beautiful stem, leaves, and bud in a pot.
The bud symbolizes the beauty of the character your Daughter is growing into.
The stem represents her strongest qualities that support her.

The bud — future wishes:

What are your wishes for your daughter's future? Consider her career, character, environment, and the people around her.

_____
_____
_____
_____
_____
_____

The leaves— Daughter's vision:

Ask your Daughter what her vision of the future is. Is it similar to what you described? In what way?

_____
_____
_____
_____
_____

The stem — strengths and advice:

What are her strongest qualities and talents that will help her have the best future?
What decision would you suggest to her to achieve the best life?

_____
_____
_____

_____
_____

Warmth of Wisdom

Daughter,
What are your Mom's strongest qualities and talents?

_____

_____

_____

How have your Mom's strong qualities influenced and helped
you become who you are today?

_____

_____

_____

Reflect with your Mom about whether there are any
commonalities in your talents and qualities, and jot down your main
thoughts.

Deck of Emotions: Shuffle and Share

Daughter and Mom. Write down different emotions on individual cards or pieces of paper—including happiness, sadness, anger, anxiety, excitement, disappointment, and surprise. Fold the cards and place them in a jar or a bowl. Shake the jar or bowl to mix up the cards. Reach in and select one card at random to see which emotion you'll reflect on.

Daughter, write the name of the emotion at the top of the table and answer the following prompts related to the emotion on your card.

Emotion / Question			
Who is someone I feel comfortable talking to when I'm feeling (emotion)?			
What could I say out loud when I'm feeling (emotion)?			
Name one thing that might trigger this emotion in you.			
Why is it important to manage this emotion carefully?			
What are some signs that this emotion is starting to overwhelm you?			

Mother, write the name of the emotion at the top of the table and answer the following prompts related to the emotion on your card.

Emotion / Question			
...o is someone I ...el comfortable ...king to when ... feeling ...notion)?			
...at could I say ... loud when I'm ...ling ...notion)?			
...ne one thing ...t might trigger ... emotion in ...			
...y is it ...portant to ...nage this ...otion ...efully?			
...at are some ...s that this ...tion is ...ting to ...rwhelm you?			

Design Your Happiness Menu

Daughter, discover and document activities that bring you joy and satisfaction, creating your personalized happiness menu. Look at the table. It is divided into four sections. "Starters" refer to brief activities lasting 5–10 minutes, designed to energize you quickly—examples include journaling or practicing yoga. "Main courses" encompass more time-consuming activities but add significant value to your day, such as visiting a park or indulging in a good book. "Sides" enhance other activities, making them more pleasurable, like listening to an audiobook at the gym. "Desserts" describes activities prone to excess, such as endlessly scrolling through social media or engaging in video games. Lastly, "Specials" highlight experiences that offer immense joy but come with a higher cost or inconvenience, like attending a concert or going shopping.

- Starters

_____ _____ _____ _____
_____ _____ _____ _____
_____ _____ _____ _____

- Main Course

_____ _____ _____ _____
_____ _____ _____ _____

- Sides

_____ _____ _____ _____
_____ _____ _____ _____

- Desserts

_____ _____ _____ _____
_____ _____ _____ _____

- Specials

_____ _____ _____ _____
_____ _____ _____ _____
_____ _____ _____ _____

Once you've got your list, share it with your Mom and check out her list too. Plan to do some of these activities together. Remember, this list is a about adding more joy and fun to your days!

Mom, discover and document activities that bring you joy and satisfaction, creating your personalized happiness menu. Look at the table. It is divided into four sections. "Starters" refer to brief activities lasting 5–10 minutes, designed to energize you quickly—examples include journaling or practicing yoga. "Main courses" encompass more time-consuming activities but add significant value to your day, such as visiting a park or indulging in a good book. "Sides" enhance other activities, making them more pleasurable, like listening to an audiobook at the gym. "Desserts" describes activities prone to excess, such as endlessly scrolling through social media or engaging in video games. Lastly, "Specials" highlight experiences that offer immense joy but come with a higher cost or inconvenience, like attending a concert or going shopping.

• Starters

_____ _____ _____ _____
_____ _____ _____ _____
_____ _____ _____ _____

• Main Course

_____ _____ _____ _____
_____ _____ _____ _____

• Sides

_____ _____ _____ _____

• Desserts

_____ _____ _____ _____

• Specials

_____ _____ _____ _____
_____ _____ _____ _____
_____ _____ _____ _____

Once you've got your list, share it with your Daughter and check out her list too. Plan to do some of these activities together. Remember, this list is all about adding more joy and fun to your days!

Shared Horizons

Look at the list of simple yet thought-provoking questions. Take turns writing answers to them. Compare your answers and reflect on them. The goal is to learn from each other, not to debate or convince. Embrace differences with curiosity.

What's your definition of success?

Mom   Daughter

_____   _____

_____   _____

_____   _____

What beliefs have you adopted from others that don't serve you now?

Mom   Daughter

_____   _____

_____   _____

_____   _____

Is it okay to lie? In what circumstances?

Mom   Daughter

_____   _____

_____   _____

_____   _____

Can money buy happiness?

Mom   Daughter

_____   _____

_____   _____

_____   _____

Do you believe in love at first sight? What makes someone fall in love?

Mom   Daughter

_____   _____
_____   _____
_____   _____

What would you choose if you could change just one thing about the world?

Mom   Daughter

_____   _____
_____   _____
_____   _____

Is it possible to have happiness without sadness?

Mom   Daughter

_____   _____
_____   _____
_____   _____

How do you think technology has changed the way we communicate with people? What are the positive and negative aspects of these changes?

Mom   Daughter

_____   _____
_____   _____
_____   _____

Evening Reflections for Confidence and Joy

Mom and Daughter,
This task is ideal for winding down your day. Reflect on a moment, no matter how small, that brought you joy, satisfaction, or pride. Try to make it a habit to take some time every evening to reflect on these prompts.

What are you proud of yourself for today?

Mom   Daughter

_____   _____
_____   _____
_____   _____
_____   _____
_____   _____
_____   _____

What are you grateful for today?

Mom   Daughter

_____   _____
_____   _____
_____   _____
_____   _____
_____   _____

I made someone else feel good when I...

Mom	Daughter
_____	_____
_____	_____
_____	_____
_____	_____
_____	_____
_____	_____

The most challenging moment of my day was ...

Mom	Daughter
_____	_____
_____	_____
_____	_____
_____	_____
_____	_____
_____	_____

In the end, think about what was similar or different in your day. How do your perspectives and emotions differ? What insights can you gain from each other's experiences?

_____

_____

_____

What is one thing you learned about each other today that you didn't know before?

_____

_____

_____

_____

Girls' Secrets

Daughter, think about the kinds of secrets you feel okay sharing with your Mom, for example, day-to-day happenings, deep feelings, or maybe future plans.

Do you believe you can tell her anything, or do you wish you could share more?

_____

_____

_____

Reflect on how much you trust your Mom to keep your secrets just between you two. What makes you feel confident that she respects your privacy? Was there a situation where you regretted telling her too much?

_____

_____

_____

Imagine telling your Mom something really personal. How would you like her to respond? Maybe just a listening ear, some comforting words, or advice?

_____

_____

_____

Is there something you've kept hidden from your Mom, perhaps from childhood? Are you now able to open up about it, and can you explain why you kept it a secret?

_____

_____

_____

Daughter, how do you consider the balance between keeping certain matters private and the importance of sharing with the key people in your life? How do your views align or differ from your Mom's on this topic?

_____

_____

_____

Mom, contemplate the types of things you're comfortable sharing with your Daughter.

Do you feel like there are more things you wish you could share with your Daughter? What's holding you back from being more open?

_____

_____

_____

Have a discussion with your Daughter at a time when you may have crossed the line with your Daughter's privacy. How did it happen, and how did you both address it? What have you learned from that experience?

_____

_____

_____

When your Daughter comes to you with personal matters, think about your initial reactions. Do you offer support, jump into problem-solving mode, or something else? What has worked well, and what could be improved?

_____

_____

_____

Are there areas in your Daughter's life you wish she would share more about? How can you create a space that encourages sharing?

_____

_____

_____

Mom, how do you consider the balance between keeping certain matters private and the importance of sharing with the key people in your life? How do your views align or differ from those of your Daughter?

_____

_____

_____

Learning Through Mistakes

Mom, take a moment to think about a recent mistake you made. It could be something small or significant in any area of your life. Share what happened. Be honest and open about the situation and how you realized it was a mistake.

_____
_____
_____
_____
_____

Discuss what you learned from this experience. How did it change your perspective or approach? What wisdom can you pass on to your Daughter from this mistake?

_____
_____
_____
_____
_____
_____

Daughter, did you make a similar mistake? How can you apply the lessons your Mom learned in your own life?

_____
_____
_____
_____
_____

Daughter, take a moment to think about a recent mistake you made. It could be something small or significant in any area of your life. Share what happened. Be honest and open about the situation and how you realized it was a mistake.

_____
_____
_____
_____
_____

Discuss what you learned from this experience. How did it change your perspective or approach? What wisdom can you pass on to your Mom from this mistake?

_____
_____
_____
_____
_____

Mom did you make a similar mistake? How can you apply the lessons your Daughter learned in your own life?

_____
_____
_____
_____

Create a keepsake:
Heartfelt Wishes

Make a special box filled with loving messages and wishes for each other. You can exchange the boxes or keep them open later, turning them into a mini time capsule.

Materials:

- A small box
- A4 paper (two pieces)
- Colored paper (preferably red or pink)
- Scissors
- Pen or marker
- Glue or heart-shaped stickers
- Ribbon

Instructions:

  - Choose a small box that will serve as the repository for your wishes and kind words. Decorate it as you like to make it more personal.
  - Cut small heart shapes from the A4 paper. Ensure they are large enough to write on but small enough to fit inside your box. Write your wishes and kind words to each other on each heart.

Follow the folding instructions to transform each heart into a small envelope:

1.Fold the lower point of the heart upwards, towards the center.

2.Fold the sides of the heart inward to form a rectangular shape.

3.Flip the envelope so the folded point is on the bottom.

4.Unfold the point you folded in the first step to create the envelope flap.

5.Fold the top part of the heart down to close the envelope.

6.Seal the envelopes with glue or a heart-shaped sticker.

-Place the sealed heart envelopes into the box. You can add as many as you like, filling the box with positive thoughts and wishes for each other.
- Tie the box with a ribbon, adding a final touch of elegance and love.

Declutter and Reflect

Daughter, set aside a time when you can peacefully go through your belongings. Create a calm and comfortable atmosphere to make this process enjoyable. Look for items with sentimental value that bring back memories and emotions.

For each treasured keepsake, write down the story of how it came into your life. Reflect on the memories or feelings it brings up and why it's special to you. Share these stories with your Mom and reflect on similar memories together.

Item	Story

After reflecting, decide which items you want to keep in your life and which ones no longer serve you and can bring happiness to someone else. Letting go of things can be a liberating experience, making room for new memories and experiences.

Mom, set aside a time to peacefully go through your belongings. Create a calm and comfortable atmosphere to make this process enjoyable. Look for items with sentimental value that bring back memories and emotions.

For each treasured keepsake, write down the story of how it came into your life. Reflect on the memories or feelings it brings up and why it's special to you. Share these stories with your Daughter and reflect on similar memories together.

Item   Story

_____   _____

_____   _____

_____   _____

_____   _____

_____   _____

_____   _____

_____   _____

_____   _____

_____   _____

_____   _____

_____   _____

_____   _____

_____   _____

After reflecting, decide which items you want to keep in your life and which ones no longer serve you and can bring happiness to someone else. Letting go of things can be a liberating experience, making room for new memories and experiences.

Book Club

Daughter, have you ever taken part in a book club or wanted to try? Now it's your opportunity to try. Pick a quote from the book that you love or a quote that you find intriguing. Write it here:

_____

_____

_____

_____

Daughter, what does this quote mean to you? What does it teach you?

_____

_____

_____

Mom, what does the quote that your Daughter picked mean to you? What does it teach you?

_____

_____

_____

Are there any books that you think your Mom should read?

_____

_____

_____

How many times a week do you currently find yourself reading? How much time each day would you like to dedicate to reading?

_____

_____

_____

_____

Mom, have you ever taken part in a book club or wanted to try? Now it's your opportunity to try. Pick a quote from the book that you love or a quote that you find intriguing. Write it here:

_____

_____

_____

_____

Daughter, what does this quote mean to you? What does it teach you?

_____

_____

_____

_____

Mom, what does the quote that your Daughter picked mean to you? What does it teach you?

_____

_____

_____

_____

Are there any books that you think Daughter should read?

_____

_____

_____

_____

How many times a week do you currently find yourself reading? How much time each day would you like to dedicate to reading?

_____

_____

_____

What would you do?

Daughter, let's explore some challenging scenarios together to better understand our values and ethical decision-making processes. Discuss your choices with your Mom, share your thoughts, and reflect on how you both make decisions based on what you think is right.

1. Imagine you unexpectedly inherit a large sum of money, making you extremely wealthy overnight. Considering your new financial status, would you choose to improve the living situations of your relatives and friends? How would you decide who to help and to what extent?

_____

_____

_____

2. A close friend shares a secret with you but asks you not to tell anyone. Later, you discover that revealing this secret could prevent harm to someone else. How do you handle the situation?

_____

_____

3. You're part of a group project, and one member isn't contributing. The deadline is approaching, and their lack of effort affects the group's performance. Do you confront them, do their part for them, or report it to the supervisor?

_____

_____

_____

4. You overhear a rumor about a colleague that could ruin their reputation and possibly cost them their job. You're not sure if the rumor is true. Do you warn them, investigate the rumor, or stay out of it?

_____

_____

5. You're offered a high-paying job at a company known for its negative impact on the environment. Taking the job would solve your financial problems, but you're concerned about the ethical implications. What's your decision?

_____

_____

_____

Mom, let's explore some challenging scenarios together to gain a deeper understanding of our values and ethical decision-making processes. Discuss your choices with your Daughter, share your thoughts, and reflect on how you both make decisions based on what you think is right.

1. Imagine you unexpectedly inherit a large sum of money, making you extremely wealthy overnight. Considering your new financial status, would you choose to improve the living situations of your relatives and friends? How would you decide who to help and to what extent?

_____

_____

_____

2. A close friend shares a secret with you but asks you not to tell anyone. Later, you discover that revealing this secret could prevent harm to someone else. How do you handle the situation?

_____

_____

_____

3. You're part of a group project, and one member isn't contributing at all. The deadline is approaching, and their lack of effort affects the group's performance. Do you confront them, do their part for them, or report it to the supervisor?

_____

_____

_____

4. You overhear a rumor about a colleague that could ruin their reputation and possibly cost them their job. You're not sure if the rumor is true. Do you warn them, investigate the rumor, or stay out of it?

_____

_____

_____

5. You're offered a high-paying job at a company known for its negative impact on the environment. Taking the job would solve your financial problems, but you're concerned about the ethical implications. What's your decision?

_____

_____

_____

The Essence of Me

Mom and Daughter, take a quiet moment to ponder the prompts below. Write down the first thing that comes to mind. There are no right or wrong answers—only your truth.

Fill in the Blanks:

I VALUE...
(things, principles, or people that are most important to you)

Mom	Daughter

I DREAM OF...
(your biggest dreams and where you see yourself in the future)

Mom	Daughter

I TAKE PRIDE IN...
(your accomplishments, qualities, or things that give you a sense of pride)

Mom	Daughter

I AM MOTIVATED BY...
(what drives you to take action and move forward in life)

Mom	Daughter

I FIND JOY IN...
(the little or big things that bring you happiness)

Mom	Daughter

I AM OFTEN FOUND...
(where people can usually find you or what you're commonly doing)

Mom	Daughter

I FEEL FULFILLED WHEN...
(the moments or achievements that give you a sense of fulfillment)

Mom	Daughter

I GET FRUSTRATED BY...
(situations or behaviors that trigger frustration in you)

Mom	Daughter

I WISH FOR...
(your hopes for yourself, your loved ones, or the world)

Mom	Daughter

I STAND FOR...
(causes or beliefs that you are passionate about and advocate for)

Mom	Daughter

My Self-Care Blueprint

Daughter, think of a time when you were your own best company. Write down your self-care practices, which help you feel refreshed and recharged. Assign them to the categories below.

Mind Moves:
   What are the things that keep your brain buzzing and happy? Could it be puzzles, drawing, or a quiet moment with a book?

_____

Body Boosts:
   Jot down your favorite ways to move and energize your body. Maybe it's stretching, walking, or dancing to your favorite tune?

_____

Soul Soothers:
   Reflect on what gives you inner peace. It could be listening to your favorite songs, spending time in nature, or writing in your journal.

_____

Growth Goals:
   Note down what you want to learn or achieve just for you. It could be a new hobby, a daily routine, a small project, a skill you want to sharpen, or just setting up a tidy workspace.

_____

_____

Reflect on the similarities and differences between your self-care practices and your Mom's. How can you both inspire and support each other in integrating these practices into your daily routines?

_____

_____

_____

_____

_____

Mother, think of a time when you were your own best company.
Write down your self-care practices, which help you feel refreshed
and recharged. Assign them to the categories below.

Mind Moves:
   What are the things that keep your brain buzzing and happy?
   Could it be puzzles, drawing, or a quiet moment with a book?

_____

_____

Body Boosts:
   Jot down your favorite ways to move and energize your body.
   Maybe it's stretching, walking, or dancing to your favorite tune?

_____

_____

Soul Soothers:
   Reflect on what gives you inner peace. It could be listening to your
   favorite songs, spending time in nature, or writing in your journal.

_____

_____

Growth Goals:
   Note down what you want to learn or achieve just for you. It
   could be a new hobby, a daily routine, a small project, a skill you
   want to sharpen, or just setting up a tidy workspace.

_____

_____

Reflect on the similarities and differences between your self-care
practices and your Daughter's. How can you both inspire and support
each other in integrating these practices into your daily routines?

_____

_____

_____

_____

_____

Who's Most Likely To?

Mom and Daughter, let's play a fun game to guess who's more likely to do certain things. This is a great way to learn more about each other and share some laughs. Here's how it works:

- One of you reads a question out loud.
- Both of you write down who you think is more likely to do the action described—either 'Mom' or 'Daughter.' If you think it's equally likely for both, write 'Both.'
- After each question, discuss why you chose your answer. It's a chance to explain your reasoning and maybe even share a story or two.

- Who's most likely to forget a birthday?
  Mom thinks:_____ Daughter thinks:_____

- Who's most likely to binge-watch a TV series in one sitting?
  Mom thinks:_____ Daughter thinks:_____

- Who's most likely to try exotic foods?
  Mom thinks:_____ Daughter thinks:_____

- Who's most likely to break into a dance in public?
  Mom thinks:_____ Daughter thinks:_____

- Who's most likely to pull a prank on someone?
  Mom thinks:_____ Daughter thinks:_____

- Who's most likely to lose their keys or phone?
  Mom thinks:_____ Daughter thinks:_____

- Who's most likely to stay calm in a stressful situation?
  Mom thinks:_____ Daughter thinks:_____

- Who's most likely to become famous?
  Mom thinks:_____ Daughter thinks:_____

- Who's most likely to go on a spontaneous adventure?
  Mom thinks:_____ Daughter thinks:_____

- Who's most likely to adopt a pet on a whim?
  Mom thinks:_____ Daughter thinks:_____

- Who's most likely to spend all day in bed?
  Mom thinks:_____ Daughter thinks:_____

- Who's most likely to get lost even with a GPS?
  Mom thinks:_____Daughter thinks: _____

- Who's most likely to cry during a sad movie?
  Mom thinks:_____Daughter thinks: _____

- Who's most likely to become a social media influencer?
  Mom thinks:_____Daughter thinks: _____

- Who's most likely to start their own business?
  Mom thinks:_____Daughter thinks: _____

- Who's most likely to sing in the shower?
  Mom thinks:_____Daughter thinks: _____

- Who's most likely to have a secret talent?
  Mom thinks:_____Daughter thinks: _____

- Who's most likely to fall asleep during a movie?
  Mom thinks:_____Daughter thinks: _____

- Who's most likely to win a cooking contest?
  Mom thinks:_____Daughter thinks: _____

- Who's most likely to read a book in one sitting?
  Mom thinks:_____Daughter thinks: _____

- Who's most likely to take up a new hobby on a whim?
  Mom thinks:_____Daughter thinks: _____

- Who's most likely to volunteer for a charity?
  Mom thinks:_____Daughter thinks: _____

- Who's most likely to run a marathon?
  Mom thinks:_____Daughter thinks: _____

- Who's most likely to become an author?
  Mom thinks:_____Daughter thinks: _____

- Who's most likely to learn a new language?
  Mom thinks:_____Daughter thinks: _____

- Who's most likely to forget an important password?
  Mom thinks:_____Daughter thinks: _____

- Who's most likely to have the most plants in their home?
  Mom thinks:_____Daughter thinks: _____

Memory Associations

Daughter, look at the list of words. Reflect on the memories associated with each word combination and write down what memories these words spark for you.

Childhood Toy
_____

Favorite Trip
_____

Best Birthday
_____

School Achievement
_____

Beloved Book
_____

Family Tradition
_____

Favorite Meal
_____

Holiday Memory
_____

Shared Hobby
_____

Special Gift
_____

Cozy Winter Day
_____

Summer Adventure
_____

Inspiring Person
_____

Unexpected Joy
_____

Act of Kindness
_____

Proud Moment
_____

Dream for the Future
_____

Review your Mom's list of memory associations. Were there any memories that surprised you or gave you a new perspective on your Mom? Also, did you notice any shared memories, and if so, do you have different recollections or feelings associated with them?

_____

_____

_____

Mom, look at the list of words. Reflect on the memories associated with each word and write down what memories this word sparks for you.

Childhood Toy
_____

Favorite Trip
_____

Best Birthday
_____

School Achievement
_____

Beloved Book
_____

Family Tradition
_____

Favorite Meal
_____

Holiday Memory
_____

Shared Hobby
_____

Special Gift
_____

Cozy Winter Day
_____

Summer Adventure
_____

Inspiring Person
_____

Unexpected Joy
_____

Act of Kindness
_____

Proud Moment
_____

Dream for the Future
_____

Review your Daughter's list of memory associations. Were there any memories that surprised you or gave you a new perspective on your Daughter? Also, did you notice any shared memories, and if so, do you have different recollections or feelings associated with them?

_____
_____
_____

Daughter, take a moment to reflect on your life's journey. Think about your childhood, your present self, and your future aspirations. Feel free to provide multiple answers to these questions. This task will help you explore who you truly are, how you've grown, and where you're headed.

Who...

Who do you feel truly understands you, and why do you feel connected to them?

_____

_____

Who would you like to reconnect with, and why have you lost touch with them?

_____

_____

When...

When did you last push yourself out of your comfort zone, and what was the outcome?

_____

_____

When have you felt the most connected to the world around you?

_____

_____

Where...

Where do you find inspiration for your dreams and aspirations?

_____

_____

Where have you felt the strongest sense of belonging, and what made it special?

_____

_____

Why...

Why is it important for you to achieve your personal goals, and how do they reflect your values?

_____

_____

Why do you think maintaining personal relationships is important in your life?

_____

_____

Mom take a moment to reflect on your life's journey. Think about your childhood, your present self, and your future aspirations. Feel free to provide multiple answers to these questions. This task will help you explore who you truly are, how you've grown, and where you're headed.

Who...
Who do you feel truly understands you, and why do you feel connected to them?

___

___

Who would you like to reconnect with, and why have you lost touch with them?

___

___

When...
When did you last push yourself out of your comfort zone, and what was the outcome?

___

___

When have you felt the most connected to the world around you?

___

___

Where...
Where do you find inspiration for your dreams and aspirations?

___

___

Where have you felt the strongest sense of belonging, and what made it special?

___

___

Why...
Why is it important for you to achieve your personal goals, and how do they reflect your values?

___

___

Why do you think maintaining personal relationships is important in your life?

___

___

Five Love Languages

Daughter, how do you share love with your family, especially your Mom?

Words of Affirmation

_____
_____
_____

Quality time

_____
_____
_____

Giving gifts

_____
_____
_____

Acts of service

_____
_____
_____

Physical Touch

_____
_____
_____

Mother, how do you share love with your family, especially your Daughter?

Words of Affirmation

_____
_____
_____

Quality time

_____
_____
_____

Giving gifts

_____
_____
_____

Acts of service

_____
_____
_____

Physical Touch

_____
_____
_____

Time Machine

Daughter, engage your Mom in a creative conversation with these questions. Feel free to add your own imaginative twist to the discussion!

If your Mom could live in another era in history or the future, which time period would she choose? What aspects of that era does she admire most?

_____

_____

_____

What fashion trends from a specific historical period would she be eager to adopt?

_____

_____

_____

Which historical figure would she be most excited to meet, and why?

_____

_____

_____

Suppose she could meet your ancestors or future descendants. What questions would she ask them?

_____

_____

_____

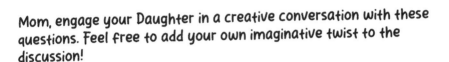

Mom, engage your Daughter in a creative conversation with these questions. Feel free to add your own imaginative twist to the discussion!

If your Daughter could live in another era in history or the future, which time period would she choose? What aspects of that era does she admire most?

_____

_____

_____

What fashion trends from a specific historical period would she be eager to adopt?

_____

_____

_____

Which historical figure would she be most excited to meet, and why?

_____

_____

_____

Suppose she could meet your ancestors or future descendants. What questions would she ask them?

_____

_____

_____

Journey's End and New Beginnings

w things did you find out about each other?

Mom	Daughter
_____	_____
_____	_____
_____	_____
_____	_____
_____	_____
_____	_____
_____	_____
_____	_____

How has the way you talk or get along with each other changed?

Mom	Daughter
_____	_____
_____	_____
_____	_____
_____	_____
_____	_____
_____	_____
_____	_____
_____	_____

After reading this journal have your thoughts about your Daughter/ Mother or her opinions changed in any way? If so, what's different now

Mom	Daughter
_____	_____
_____	_____
_____	_____
_____	_____
_____	_____
_____	_____
_____	_____
_____	_____

Mom and Daughter,

What do you want to do with this journal once you're done with it?

_____

_____

_____

Who will take care of this journal as a keepsake?

_____

Consider choosing a future date to revisit this journal together.
Setting a reminder for this date can help ensure you both come back
to reflect on your journey and see how things have evolved.

Date we finished this journal: _____

Date we plan to revisit it: _____

101

Made in United States
Orlando, FL
13 November 2024